how and when to

DECLUTTER

A Simple Guide

Andrew Ware

www.howandwhentodeclutter.com

© 2019 Andrew Ware

All inquiries should be made to the author: www.howandwhentodeclutter.com

Disclaimer

The material in this publication is of the nature of general comment only, and doe: not represent professional advice. It is not intended to provide specific guidance for particular circumstances and it should not be relied on as the basis for any decision to take action or not take action on any matter that it covers. To the maximum extent permitted by law, the author disclaims all responsibility and liability to any person, arising directly or indirectly from any person taking or not taking action based on the information in this publication.

ISBN 978-0-6485791-0-6

CONTENTS

FOREWORD

For as long as I can remember, I've been the 'neat one' or the 'clean one' or the 'oh my goodness, your house looks like a display home' one (when I was single!).

Coupled with that, when at home, work or at friends' houses, when I do my housework, when I've moved house or I've helped friends move house, I look at things and think, *Does that need to be kept?*, *Why is that being kept?*, *This can be much neater*, or, *This could be decluttered and make a much nicer space!*

It recently occurred to me that I could share these thoughts in a practical way, and this simple guide is the result of that.

The HOW section will take you through each room with a guide of how to declutter, and the WHEN section suggests stages that occur during our lifetime when it is best to declutter.

All the best decluttering.

Andrew

DEFINITIONS

House, Apartment, Bungalow, Unit

I will use the term 'house' throughout this guide, but whenever I mention 'house', you can substitute it for the type of domicile you live in.

Room or Section

I will use the term 'room', and for the most part I will be talking about a whole room. But, especially in small apartments, you can substitute it to also mean section.

YOUR DECLUTTER LEVEL

Knowing where you are on the 'Declutter Scale' (if there were such a thing), is a great place to start.

Declutter Level 1

Readers at this level are people like me who *are* decluttered. *However*, it might just remind you that there are other people out there in the world who live decluttered lives (so you're not so weird after all). And hopefully there's something in this guide that you can add to your repertoire of decluttering.

Declutter Level 2

Readers at this level, well, you are my primary audience.

Maybe you've come to my guide directly. You've come to the realisation that your house is on its way to, or already has become, a disaster zone and something needs to be done about it. You've actively sought out a guide to help you declutter.

Or maybe you've come to my guide indirectly. In your subconscious you knew your house was, or is, getting out of hand and then, out of the blue, someone mentions this guide and your subconscious tells you that's what you need. Maybe a fellow Declutter Level 2 person gives or lends you their copy. Or maybe a Declutter Level 1 friend or family member has bought this guide for you because they feel you would really benefit from reading it.

In any case, if you are willing to begin decluttering, it stands to reason that you will achieve that goal with the help of this guide.

Declutter Level 3

Readers at this level could have their house featured on the TV show *Hoarders*!

Now, before you close this guide for good, I'm glad it has reached your hands, I genuinely am. The decluttering process for you will be hardest, but I truly believe that in the end, a decluttered house will be immensely more pleasurable than a cluttered house.

On a serious note, there may be an underlying psychological issue that needs to be dealt with. My guide will help you get your house decluttered; a psychologist will help you get your mind decluttered. There is absolutely no shame in seeking help for what is probably a genuine mental illness you may have.

INTRODUCTION

We all have items in our houses that needlessly take up space. Some of it has sentimental value, like the trophy you won that year in that sport you used to play, and some of it, well, why do you have a funny-looking rock sitting on the shelf? When did it get there? Where did it come from? Why do you still have it? The idea of decluttering is to work out what needs to be kept and what doesn't.

Decluttering gives you, your family and your house some breathing room. Let's make this easy. Do you feel more relaxed thinking about a house that will feature on the TV show *Better Homes and Gardens*, or do you feel more relaxed thinking about a house that would be on the TV show *Hoarders*? (I'm hoping you said *Better Homes and Gardens*!)

This guide isn't about 'spring cleaning'; that is, taking up a weekend (or multiple weekends) or a week of your time to clean the whole house *at once*. I don't want you to feel overwhelmed by the task of decluttering. Decluttering should be a positive and regulated experience.

I've broken decluttering down to three steps:

Throw It. Sort It. Clean It.

To be honest, '**Throw It**' and '**Clean It**' I can cover in one sentence: throw out your rubbish and give your house a clean. (I will, however, go into more detail on these.) '**Sort It**' will require a bit more work.

And speaking of work, let's get started!

STEP 1: THROW IT

This will be the quickest and easiest of the steps, so it's a good starting point. Hopefully you'll only collect one garbage bag or less of rubbish for the whole house. If you've got a feeling that it might require a few garbage bags, then I would suggest doing one room or one section of your house at a time.

Getting rid of the rubbish first is the no-brainer part of the steps. You know what rubbish is. You know where it belongs. Rubbish doesn't require you to think whether you need it or not ... it's rubbish! It's what the garbage collectors pick up weekly.

But, just in case you think this is a trick question, think of rubbish this way: if a friend or family member where to drop in unannounced, what are the items around the house that really should be in the bin? I know, I know, it sounds like I'm talking down to you ... I'm not. It's just really easy to say, 'I'll take care of that later,' and then when friends or family pop round you realise you've got a whole garbage bag full of 'I'll take care of that later.'

For most people, sorting their rubbish into recyclable and non-recyclable is, again, a no-brainer, so please do that. For some of you Level 2s—and definitely Level 3s—this step may be overwhelming in and of itself. If that is you, then please try to recycle, but if you can't, just throw the recyclables out with the other rubbish. I need you to learn how to throw items out. If there are hurdles in your way of doing that, then they need to be taken away (because there will be things harder for you to throw out in the '**Sort It**' step).

So you're throwing the rubbish out. You've picked up that bottle that's been sitting around for a few days. That bit of paper that was in the corner that you were going to get around to picking up and then forgot about. You've looked under the couch. 'Oh! Some coins.' You've found a, 'Well, I'm not sure what it is, it's a bit of plastic that's broken off something.' It gets thrown out!

At the end of '**Throw It**', hopefully you've got less than or just one bag of rubbish to throw out. If, however, there's no way you're going to fit all the rubbish into your bin for the weekly garbage collection, there are a few solutions.

1) On the next bin night, go around to your neighbours' houses. Introduce yourself, if you don't know them already, and tell them about this guide that is helping you declutter your house. Tell them you've got some garbage bags you need to get rid of. Ask them if they wouldn't mind if you put some in their bins. Hopefully, they'll say yes and you're onto **Step 2**.

2) Maybe a month of bin pickups wouldn't get rid of the garbage you've just collected in your house. In that case you might need a trailer. If you've got one, great. If you need one, either borrow a friend's or, if you can't drive with a trailer, rope your friend into helping you take it to the tip. If you're a rate payer, some councils give you tip tokens—use one. Or, if you don't have tokens, well, you're just going to have to pay cash! And remember, if you needed a friend to help you go to the tip, make sure and shout them lunch or coffee or a beer, because, just between you and me, you may need them after **Step 2** and now is a good time to butter them up.

3) Some councils who don't have tips offer a curb-side pickup service. Don't be surprised if some of your neighbours take advantage of you getting rid of rubbish by putting a few things in the pile too. At least you're getting rid of what you need to get rid of.

Whichever method you choose, get rid of the rubbish as soon as possible. You need to break the cycle of leaving items around the house, and getting rid of the garbage is the start of that. Also, you are about to go to **Step 2**, which will require a lot more items to be thrown out.

STEP 2: SORT IT

Rule #1

'Have I used it in the last 12 months?

Am I going to use it in the next 12 months?'

Rule #2

'Is it going into the garbage,

into your garage sale,

to the op shop, or is it staying?'

This guide is based on two rules. **Rule #1** is a great rule I use to decide whether or not an item is going to stay or if it's going to go. Then **Rule #2** gives each item a designation. It's going to go into the garbage, OR it's going to go into your garage sale, OR it's going to the op shop, OR it's going to stay.

Is it Garbage?

Well, you've had practice with this one already. You got rid of the garbage that was easy to identify as garbage. Now you're going to get rid of the rest of the garbage. By 'rest of the garbage' I mean things like: candles that have lost their ability to shed any more light; pens that have run out of ink; books that have pages ripped out of them; Christmas, birthday, thank you cards (or any card that has overstayed its required allotted time); anything that is broken and wouldn't even sell at a garage sale, such as printers, toys, DVDs and CDs that don't play anymore (I might be showing my age here—how about I add cassettes to the list?); USB drives that no longer work; puzzles or board games with missing pieces. You get the idea. Items that camouflage themselves from being garbage but are, in fact, just that ... garbage.

Will it Sell?

It's preferable to set up an area outside (and under cover if possible) where you can temporarily store items for your garage sale. 'Wait, what?' I hear you say. 'A garage sale?' Yes, a garage sale. You're going to make some money off of all those items you've had sitting around your house, or at least try to make some money.

'I could sell it on eBay,' I hear you say with excitement. Well, yes you could, but are you really going to get more for it selling it online? Are you really going to go to all the hassle of setting up a listing and waiting for it to sell for a second-hand item that probably won't sell anyway? How do your items compare to not only second-hand items, but to similar brand-new items that are for sale online? My guess is that the garage sale is going to give you the most that these items are worth.

If you go to the effort of making a listing, and go to the effort of waiting for the listing to sell or not sell, you've just given the item/s 'value'. You've spent time on them, so now they owe you something. You've put effort in for them, and you want that effort paid back. You have given them (artificial) value, and why would you get rid of something that has value? So, I recommend just putting them in the garage sale pile instead.

The other reason I don't want you to sell these items online is because I want them out of your house; I want them gone. They've sat around collecting dust and cluttering up your house long enough. I don't want you to give yourself an excuse to keep them around longer. That's the benefit of setting up an area outside of the house. Once these items are outside, they don't come back in.

For the apartment dwelling declutterers, it's a little bit harder. I'm hoping you have a balcony you could use to temporarily store your items (making sure they don't get wet). If you don't, you'll need to set up a space inside instead. As much as possible, make sure that the space isn't in the way of your everyday living. By that I mean, keep it out of the way of your most heavily trafficked areas. You don't want to be tripping over the items all the time.

Also, the other hurdle for apartment dwellers is the ability to have a garage sale. You will have to contact your local council to see if they allow selling on the footpath. Another option is to join a car boot sale or 'Sunday' market for just one day. If none of these options are available to you (and you haven't found another solution), your items will go to garbage and the op shop.

Is it Worthy of the Op Shop?

Maybe having a garage sale isn't your thing. Or maybe you'd prefer a charity to make a little money off of your items. If this is the case, then you're going to be taking them to the op shop.

There is a slight difference though as to items that are right for a garage sale and items that are worthy for an op shop. To know whether items should be donated to an op shop, there is only one question you need to ask yourself: 'If I was shopping at an op shop, would I buy it?' That means: are the items clean, undamaged and of good quality? If your items tick these three boxes, they are worthy of being donated to an op shop. If your items don't tick these three boxes, then they either go into your garage sale or to the tip. (On a side note, some op shops don't accept electrical goods, or items of an electrical nature, so dispose of them at a tip.)

Are You Going to Keep It?

You've decided your items aren't garbage. You've decided not to sell them. You've decided not to give them to an op shop. It therefore means they are going to stay. This is where I'm going to delve into each room and help you decide whether what you're left with is really worth keeping, or if it's worth getting rid of.

Throughout this guide, I'll simply be referring to the rules as **Rule #1** and **Rule #2**. If you forget what they are, or which rule is which, you can pop back to this section or flick to the last page of the book, where I've put them as well.

LET'S START

The fridge, pantry and medicine cabinet are the three sections I recommend to do first. They are easy. They are quick. And they give you an overview of the whole process in a short amount of time.

Fridge

Well, **Rule #1** shouldn't apply here and there's only one part of **Rule #2** that we need to worry about and that is: 'Is it going into the garbage?' Yes, it is.

Let's start with the crisper (or vegetable) drawer. Throw out the brown lettuce, the bendy carrots, the dry mushrooms and whatever else is in there that you've totally forgotten about.

Next, it's onto the items that are past their best-before or use-by date. You have a little bit of leeway if the items have just gone out of date (I'll leave that up to you). But you know what needs to be thrown out and now is the time to do that.

Don't forget your freezer. Is there anything right at the back that you've forgotten about? Is there anything that's been in there so long that it's got freezer burn? Anything you know you're not going to eat? Throw it out.

This is also a good time to go through your garage fridge, if you have one. If it's literally your 'beer' fridge, then job done. If, however, you keep food in it, well, find anything that needs to be thrown out and do so.

To finish off the fridge, now's a good time to sort out all those magnets you have on it. (I mean, you're standing there, so we might as well take care of them now!)

For the most part, the magnets you have are probably from a local politician who slapped his face on a calendar and put it in your letterbox. And it's not even from this year. It was a few years back (and possibly a few moves back), but you never took it off the fridge. Or, it's a magnet from that great takeaway shop you went to every Friday night, but you no longer live in that area. Or, it's a magnet from Hawaii and you haven't even been to Hawaii!

Take a quick moment now to declutter the magnets. Keep a few because you're always going to need a few (and, truth be told, there's probably another one on its way to your letterbox from your new local politician).

Pantry

For the most part, the pantry will be the same as the fridge (except less cold!).

Once again, as you go through each item, what has gone past its expiry date? What will you never use? For those of you on diets, what shouldn't be in your pantry, but is?

Take a look as well at what is on the top shelf. For the most part, this is a 'storage shelf' because it's high up. Is there anything up there that doesn't need to be? Is there anything that can go in your garage sale? Is there anything that can go to the op shop?

Medicine Cabinet

I don't mind advising throwing out over-the-counter medicines because they can be replaced easily. You throw out that bottle of cough medicine that's months past its use-by date, and suddenly after decluttering your house you come down with a cough. Well, you can just pop down to your local chemist or even the supermarket to pick up a bottle. However, be careful of any prescription medications you have. If it relates to anything recent, I would suggest keeping it, and then the next time you declutter, it might then be time to throw it out. But if you have a packet of (whatever 12-letter word is its name) that was prescribed for you for that medical incident or operation you had five years ago (and it's well past its use-by date), well, it's probably safe to say that it should be thrown out.

Result

Look at what you've just accomplished. You've decluttered three areas and it didn't even take that long. Be proud of your accomplishment. Now it's time to move on to the rest of the house, with **Rule #1** and **Rule #2** firmly in mind.

THE ROOMS

I've set this section up alphabetically. Feel free to start at the front end of the house and end up at the back end. Or, start at the back end of the house and end up at the front end. Maybe do the lounge room and kitchen first, and then move on to the kids' rooms. Or do the kids' rooms first and then move on to the lounge room and kitchen—whatever suits you.

I personally suggest starting at the lounge room, kitchen, master bedroom or master bathroom/ensuite; the areas you are always in. And because you are always in these rooms, the enjoyment of being in a decluttered room should get you through the rest of the house. (I tend to leave the kids' rooms to last because they generally don't care how their rooms look!)

Pick a room from the list, and after you've completed decluttering it, jump ahead to **Step 3: Clean It**. Once you've read and completed that step for the room you are in, come back to this section and move on to decluttering your next room.

The great thing about this guide is that at this point you've got all you need to declutter your house. You've got the **three steps** and you've got **Rule #1** and **Rule #2**. You could stop reading, continue decluttering the rest of your house and live happily (decluttered) ever after! (You do know I want you to read the rest of the book at some stage though, right?)

Spend a minimum of an hour a day (which is the bare minimum, I should add) decluttering, and you will be surprised at how much you can get done. If finding an hour a day *is* a challenge, might I suggest skipping the hour-long news programs, or skip an hour of book reading, gaming, etc. There are plenty of areas in your life that you could find a wasted hour. Put it to good use; put it to decluttering.

Bathroom/Ensuite

You've already done your medicine cabinet (if it's in this room). Next are your bathroom cupboards. And what a shemozzle they can be!

Maybe there are spare towels, rolls of toilet paper, soap (spare soap), shampoo (spare shampoo), makeup, feminine hygiene products, lotions, gels, toothpastes, toothbrushes, floss (other dental products), shavers, shaving products, hairbrushes, hairdryer, hair straightener, hair colour kits, perfumes, mirror or mirrors ... I think I'll stop there!

Again, throw out anything that has made its way back into the cupboard when it should have been thrown out already. Next is anything that you will never use: old makeup, old razors, maybe those scented soaps that Grandma gave you. Even if you didn't know soap could be made with that scent and because Grandma gave it to you, you don't want to throw it out! If it's not going to be used, **Rule #2** it.

Bookcases

My wife and kids are bookworms, so we have plenty to fill our bookcases. Your aim with a bookcase is to not have it overflow. 'Overflow?' I hear you say. 'How can you overflow a bookcase?' I'm glad you asked!

Look at one shelf on your bookcase. From left to right with books standing on their bottoms, that is how many books should fit on that one shelf. But, there is usually a difference in depth between the bookcase itself and the books. This is where a lot of the time, in this space, books are laid down on their front (or back). And that's how you overflow your bookcase, and that's how you clutter a bookcase. Your goal is to declutter.

So it's time to look at those books. What have you read once and know you will never read again? What have you read half of and know you will never read the other half because it was so bad? Why do you have that old series still? Why do you still have kids' books on the shelf when your kids are now at uni and there is no prospect of them giving you grandchildren anytime soon!

E-readers give you a huge advantage in this area. You can have a hundred books or even a thousand books in the palm of your hand. Let me give you an idea. Books you absolutely love, keep the physical copy. Books that you like (or maybe tolerate), keep them on your e-reader.

Sort out whether your books are going into the recycling, into your garage sale, or to the op shop. Or are they staying because you do read them over and over again and they are 'worthy' of remaining in the bookcase?

CDs/DVDs

I'm just going to write 'ditto' (to the bookcases) and we're done.

Clothes (Walk-In-Wardrobe, Drawers or Cupboards)

Let's face a fact: there are a limited amount of clothes you can wear in one day. Multiply that by seven and that is the maximum amount of clothes you can wear in a week. Now, have a guess at how many weeks of clothes you currently have in your walk-in-wardrobe, or your cupboards and drawers.

Rule #1 in this room is so easy (I only have to change one of the words). 'Have I worn it in the last 12 months? Am I going to wear it in the next 12 months?' And before all you smart alecs pipe up with 'my girlfriend / wife / partner is pregnant so we can't get rid of some clothes', I'll redirect you to the second part of **Rule #1**: 'Am I going to wear it in the *next* 12 months?' Of course, there are exceptions, but what I want you to look at is the *excess* of your clothes.

The easiest clothes to sort are the ones you know you aren't going to wear again. Or those socks with the holes in them that you keep just in case you run out of socks, to which I say buy more socks or do your washing more often. Once you get past the easy items, move on to the harder ones. Do you need all those t-shirts? Do you need all those shirts? Do you need all those trousers? Do you need all those jeans? Do you need all those dresses? Do you need all those skirts? Do you need all those bras? Do you need all that underwear?

I'm definitely not saying to just have seven days' worth of clothes available to wear. What you need to ask yourself is, 'Do I have an excess amount of clothes that are cluttering up the space?'

Since you're applying **Rule #1** and **Rule #2** to your clothes, this is the time to get rid of more garbage. You thought you'd already gotten rid of all the garbage, didn't you? Well, there is garbage hanging right in front of your eyes, unused coat hangers.

Some people prefer to keep their clothes in drawers. I prefer to hang mine up. It probably won't surprise you that I have the exact number of coat hangers for the amount of clothes I have. 'But what if you buy something and you need another coat hanger?' Well, my wife has a couple of extra coat hangers on her side of our walk-in-wardrobe, so if I do need one, I can grab one from there. There's really no point in keeping a stack of unused coat hangers. I would recommend keeping just five extra. Why only five? Well, I doubt you're buying clothes every weekend and therefore don't need a pile of unused coat hangers taking up space. I would imagine that months will pass by the time you use up those spare five. Also, you can practically get a 10 or 12 pack of coat hangers for next to nothing *anywhere!*

Entry/Hallway

My guess is, walking into your house and having a decluttered entry is going to feel much better than walking into your house and having a cluttered entry. Whatever sort of decorative setup you have, keep it super simple; this will help keep it continually decluttered. If you have the space, I would also suggest putting in a shoe rack. Whether it's a rack or a box or a basket setup, a bunch of shoes look much neater put away than randomly sitting in the way of the front door.

Gaming Centre

For the most part, decluttering the gaming centre doesn't take up that much time.

First, are there any consoles or controllers that are broken? Are there any batteries or battery packs that no longer work? Are there any cartridge games (for the older consoles) that no longer work? Are there any game discs that are so scratched that they no longer work? These things are garbage. Yep, you've got more garbage hiding in plain sight. If they don't work, throw them out.

The consoles themselves are (probably) already going to be on a shelf in the TV unit. Hopefully the unit has a backing (like a bookshelf) with cable holes so you can feed the power cables through them. Hiding the cables makes up the majority of decluttering the gaming centre.

If you have multiples of the same gaming console, now's a good time to ask why. If there's no good reason, then maybe the multiples need to go. If you also have different gaming consoles, are you still using all of them? It would be a good time to apply **Rule #1** to them.

To complete the declutter of the gaming centre, you can choose one drawer for the controllers and extra battery packs and another drawer or a bookcase for the games. Obviously, the amount of space you need for the games is going to depend on how many there are. Organise the games in console order (if you have more than one console) and have the game cases face the same way however they are stored. If you want to go 'full declutter', organise the games in alphabetical order.

Kids' Art

Finger paintings. Crayon drawings. Ice-cream stick creations. Pipe cleaner animals. And many, many, many other pieces of artwork that kids bring home over the years. I'm not suggesting throwing it all out, but what I will suggest is to drastically declutter what you keep. (Obviously, the more kids you have, the stricter you're going to have to be.)

Chances are you've got some of the kids' art on the fridge, and chances are that the available space on the fridge is only enough to hold one or two pieces. The kids probably also have some of their art on their bedroom walls. The easiest way to declutter is: as new pieces of art arrive, the old pieces are removed. It's a one-to-one ratio. This system will keep your art clutter down.

When it comes to keeping art long term, like their first finger painting, or their first drawing of the family (in all its stick figure glory!), there's no harm in storing it away, but you need to be *very* selective. For example, if you have one kid, from kindergarten to grade six, if you took the best art piece from every year, you'll end up with seven pieces of art. If you have two kids, the total will be 14. No matter how many kids you have, the amount of art can pile up quickly, and all it's doing is cluttering up your home.

For our kids' art, we have an A3 poster-sized under-bed plastic container (that was purchased from a hardware store), and it's only 15 cm high. This enables us to be selective of what we keep because the height of the container restricts us.

Kids' Bedroom/s

We've just discussed the kids' art, and I discuss the kids' toys a little further in the guide, so what's left are the kids' clothes.

Much like your own clothes, ask yourself, 'How many clothes can they actually wear in a week?' My guess is you probably have an excess of kids' clothes, but there is a really simple (and I think great!) way of decluttering their clothes. This solution is also a great money saver if you have more than one kid.

Throughout this guide, I've intentionally refrained from suggesting you purchase anything to help in your decluttering process. But this is where I will break this rule. Go to your local supermarket or hardware store and buy some containers with lids. (I'd suggest something like 35L or 50L, but the size will depend on how many excess clothes you have and how much space you have to store them.) Then, all you need to do is separate the clothes by size, and each container will be one size. You can, however, usually get away with all the baby items in one container—so from the smallest size to size one or two—but then after that each size has its own container. Of course, use your own judgement here. Sizes three and four might also fit in the same container together. However, I would suggest limiting each container to only two sizes.

The great thing about this system is that it declutters the kids' rooms, if the kids ruin their clothes you have some spares, and you've got an immediate source of hand-me-downs as the kids get older. If you decide you want to space the kids' ages apart, as the oldest grows out of clothes you just store them away, and once the next kid comes along, you've got an immediate source of clothes.

Finally, all you need now is a space to store the containers. You can do that in the garage or in the shed, or if you've cleared some space in the linen or laundry cupboards, you could store them there. Because they aren't going to be accessed too much, I'd put them somewhere where they will be out of mind and out of sight.

Kitchen Cupboards

How many cupboards you have obviously depends on the size of your kitchen, but I will break them down to: bakeware, kitchen appliances, pots and pans, and tableware. And the dreaded plastics cupboard!

The bakeware, kitchen appliances, and pots and pans cupboards shouldn't take you that long. These cupboards have only a few items taking up the space. Is there anything that is so old you don't use, or so old that you shouldn't be using? Do you have five of the same size baking tray and you only ever use one or two at a time? Do all your pans and saucepans have their lids? If you have random lids that are never going to be used, maybe it's time to apply **Rule #2** to them. Do you still have the old blender (with all those attachments) that your parents handed down to you (you know, the one you used as a kid!) that you have never ever used and will never ever use? Or, if you did want to blend, you'd buy a new one anyway. Maybe it's time to apply **Rule #1** and **Rule #2** to it.

The tableware cupboard should also be pretty quick to do. Is there anything that has chips or cracks? Probably best to throw them out. Are there any 'randoms' in the cupboard? And what I mean by that is left over tableware from previous sets. There's usually not many of them, but for the sake of keeping everything the same (I like when everything matches, even my tableware!), maybe it's time to throw them out. My guess is you've probably got a good collection of mugs, cups and glasses. It's a good time to ask yourself whether you really need all of them. Might be time to apply **Rule #1** and **Rule #2** to some of them so you're no longer squeezing them into the cupboard.

Now, to the dreaded plastics cupboard! What you need to do here is make a space on the bench or meals table and take everything, yes everything, out of the plastics cupboard and put them onto the space you've cleared. Match all the containers with their lids. If there are any containers without lids, or any lids without containers, then apply **Rule #2** to them. For the most part, the mismatching items you'll probably throw out. Also, look for plastic items that are well past their 'use-by date': the ones that have been through the dishwasher accidentally and are a bit warped; or the ones that you could never get the pasta stains out of. If you have a container that you never use because it's always hard to put the lid on it, rather than keeping it because 'it's still a good container', throw it out. If it's not doing its job then it's not worth keeping.

Kitchen Drawers

Your top drawer is probably cutlery. The next is probably utensils. You might then have a drawer that has garbage bags, cling wrap, aluminium foil, baking paper and sandwich bags. And then 'that' drawer. (Well, at least one of them will be 'that' drawer!) By 'that' I mean the 'miscellaneous' drawer. It's the drawer that ends up with all the bits and pieces that either don't actually belong anywhere else in the house, or you've been too lazy to put them back where they belong. But, first, let's tackle the cutlery drawer.

This is the part of the guide that will definitely make me sound crazy! Open your cutlery drawer. Do you have too much cutlery? Yes, you read that correctly. With the cutlery that you have on hand, do you have the ability to serve a 10-course meal for 10 people and not run out of cutlery? If the answer is yes, then maybe you have too much. (Unless, of course, you do serve 10-course meals for 10 people every weekend, then you should be fine!) If you think you might have too much cutlery (and there aren't too many places that I actually suggest this), put a quarter or a half or three-quarters of it in a bag and put it in one of the cupboards. If after three or six months you haven't needed that 'extra' cutlery, then I suggest applying **Rule #2** to it. If you haven't used it, then it's clearly just taking up space.

The next drawer is the utensils. Bottle openers, tongs, skewers, whisks, spatulas, wooden spoons. Again, how many of each of these do you actually need? Go through your utensils drawer and take out what you *think* you don't need. Put those items in the bag with the extra cutlery, and if you haven't used them in the timeframe you've allotted, then I again suggest applying **Rule #2** to them.

Here's a good test if you're not sure whether you've got too many utensils in the drawer. When you open the drawer, if you have to regularly put your hand in and manoeuvre what's in it to actually get the drawer open, then you've got too much in there!

Your next drawer is either a second utensils drawer or maybe it has things like garbage bags, cling wrap and baking paper. For the most part, you won't need to do much with this drawer. Maybe just look at how many freezer bags you have. Have you managed to collect a large amount? I don't know how they do it but freezer bags seem to multiply! You only need one pack. In fact, you probably only need half a pack. Those freezer bags last forever.

And, finally, onto 'that' drawer. First off, throw out anything that is rubbish. Second, if there is anything in there that belongs elsewhere—such as batteries, or any type of stationery, any small tools (or screws or nails), or any sewing items—put them back where they belong. If what is left doesn't belong elsewhere, does it pass **Rule #1**? Then apply **Rule #2**. If after **Rule #2** it ends up staying, then that's where it belongs.

I've used four drawers as a basis; your kitchen may have more than four. In any case, simply run through the process above for every drawer.

Linen Cupboard

It's quite easy to let a linen cupboard get out of hand. You find yourself stuffing and pushing the linen in because, let's face it, it's pretty flexible. The other problem is that linen cupboards tend to be deep and the shelves tend to be high. By stuffing and pushing, you can actually get quite a lot in there. But as declutterers, that's not our goal.

Let's say you have four winter blankets in the linen cupboard. **Rule #1**: 'Have I used all four winter blankets in the last 12 months?' Well, no actually. I only ever use just the one because it's my favourite and it does an incredible job. Also, the kids' doonas are warm enough and they never need extra blankets. Apply **Rule #2** to the extra blankets. Do you have spare pillows in the cupboard? The ones that are really flat and were replaced but you didn't want to throw them out. Maybe it's time to apply **Rule #1** and **Rule #2** to them. Do you have an old doona in the cupboard? I'm sorry to have to bring this up, but is it yellow from all the years of sweat? (Ewww, disgusting!) Apply **Rule #2** to it now! Or maybe it's as simple as sheet sets you no longer use because you've changed the colour scheme of your house.

Again, spare sheet sets, pillows, doonas and blankets are handy to have, especially if you have friends and family stay over a lot. A good question is: 'Would I want to sleep in a bed that is made up of my spare linen?'

The other items that take up space in the linen cupboard are the towels. In our house we have two towels each for showering. (As there are four of us, that's eight towels, but, remember, four are always on towel racks.) We have one beach/pool towel for each kid, one camp towel for each kid, two spare shower towels for guests, and four used/work towels (for cleaning, etc.) Have a look at the amount of towels you have and work out which ones need **Rule #1** and **Rule #2** applied to them.

Lounge Room

Now, don't laugh. Do you have furniture you don't need? (I told you not to laugh!) Is there a bean bag in your lounge room that barely gets used? Yeah, it's nice to sit on it now and again, sometimes the dog takes a seat in it. Sometimes the kids play with it (while you sit there hoping it doesn't finally burst open). If it's not being used regularly, then maybe it doesn't need to be there at all.

Do you have those stackable side tables but only ever use the biggest one? Then maybe it's time to apply **Rule #2** to the smaller ones.

Have you got a spare couch in your lounge room? You know, the one a mate gave to you and you thought, *Why not? It's free.* But no one really sits on it. Apply **Rule #1** and **Rule #2** to it.

A lot of the time, the bigger furniture doesn't even get acknowledged when decluttering takes place, but it needs to be. Furniture takes up the biggest amount of space, so it's only fair to ask whether it *needs* to be taking up that space.

Master Bedroom

For the most part, your bedroom will consist of a bed (I hope!), bedside tables, probably a TV, and for your clothes, drawers, a closet, or a walk-in robe. I've already covered clothes earlier on, so let's look at the bedside tables.

To be honest, your bedside table and its drawers shouldn't have that much on/in them. You might keep a lamp and/or alarm clock on top, but in the drawers themselves, maybe the bedroom TV remote, a sleep mask, a book, tissues, a pen, a pair of glasses, your watch, hair tie, or ear phones.

What bedside table drawers generally are though, are 'that drawer', just like a kitchen's 'that drawer' that we talked about earlier. They're filled with every random thing imaginable, which leads them to just being a junk drawer. You have an extra task (in addition to **Rule #1** and **Rule #2**) with your bedside table drawer. Put the items back where they belong. The half-used packet of medication goes back into your medicine cabinet. That loose battery gets put back with your other batteries. The loose change either goes into your wallet or into your change jar. The random makeup and cosmetics that you've just thrown in there, put them back in your makeup case (or wherever you keep them). The books you're not reading go on the bookcase. The 10 pens you've collected, they go back to wherever you keep your stationery.

After you've decluttered your bedside table drawers, your closet shelves or your walk-in-wardrobe shelves are next. They tend to be used for long-time storage items, such as suitcases, photo albums (showing my age again!), bags, hats, maybe a small instrument that you used to play, that box of Christmas decorations. For the most part, these items will pass **Rule #1**, but it's still worth seeing if each item does, and if there is anything that doesn't, then apply **Rule #2** to them.

Finally in the master bedroom, I want to talk about what's under your bed. (No, not the monsters!) If it's 'nothing' because your bed base goes to the floor, then, job done! If you have one of those beds that lifts up to reveal storage compartments (usually for spare blankets and doonas) then you'll declutter that section pretty quickly. If, however, you have the availability of 'storage space' under your bed, I would recommend using it for one or two items, and only if you have absolutely no other place for those one or two items to go. Under the bed is a bit like the bedside table drawers. Items get put under there and then more items, and then eventually there's a pile of items under the bed that get forgotten about, and if it's forgotten about, is it something you really need to keep anyway? Making a rule (if you have to) of only keeping one or two items under your bed, will ensure that it remains decluttered.

Photos

You probably won't be surprised when I say there are no photos or paintings hanging up on the walls of my house. Some of you do like to have photo frames and pictures and paintings hanging up. The only advice I can give here is: the less you put up, the less cluttered the wall will be and the less closed in the room will feel.

Rumpus Room

Ah, yes, the rumpus room. This one is a little bit tricky but we'll get through it!

The first question is: what is the purpose of your rumpus room? The second question is: is it serving that purpose? For example, if for the last 20 years the kids have been using the rumpus room but now they've gone to uni or have moved out, and the rumpus room is now just a pool and table tennis table storage area, then it's not serving its purpose. It might be time to give it a new purpose, like a gym or maybe a retreat where your friends or family can stay over. Maybe you could set it up as a reading room, or maybe get some indoor plants and set up a nice green area inside the house.

However, if you don't know what its new purpose is going to be, there's no real harm in leaving the room as it is ... well, almost! Read on.

If your rumpus room is serving its purpose, let me assume you have one or more of these in it: pool/billiard table, table tennis table, dart board, bar, bean bag/s, TV and gaming centre, kids' toys, exercise equipment.

The trick with the rumpus room is to ask the question: does each item have enough space around so it can be used without any hindrance? Can a game of pool be played without a pool stick hitting the wall? Can a game of darts be played with enough area around it so just in case a dart veers off course, it doesn't go into someone's head! Can table tennis be played without tripping over a bean bag? Can you get on and off the exercise bike without having to squeeze between the TV and the kids' toys? Look at what space you've got and fill it accordingly. If you do have a problem with space, then apply **Rule #1** to each item. It will make you realise how little or how much you are using what's in the room and then you can declutter the room accordingly.

Toilet

For those of you who put up calendars or posters, maybe just do an update. If you want a calendar, make sure it's the current year, and if you put up posters, make sure they're still relevant. For example, if it's a times table poster that you put up when the kids were in primary school and now they are in high school, I think it's time that it could come down. If it's a poster of an animal doing something funny, is it still funny or has the joke lost its effectiveness?

Toys

Kids' toys; the bane of any parent's existence! I'm going to share a great piece of wisdom with you: kids do not need the amount of toys that they have.

Every parent knows (or if you don't, start taking notice) that kids have one, two or three absolute favourite toys that they play with. They play with those things every. Single. Day. Sometimes it shows with the amount of wear and tear they have on them. Everything else is clutter. Your task is to first work out what their absolute favourites are, and this should be pretty easy. The next task is to work out what the next one or two favourites are. Your final task is to apply **Rule #2** to the other 50 to 75 per cent.

My one directive here is this: *Do not* do this in front of them! Do not ask *them* if you can apply **Rule #2** to their toys. That toy that they haven't seen or played with for ages, will suddenly become their favourite thing that they can't live without. If you then apply **Rule #2** to it, you might just be asking for a tantrum.

You also need to cover your tracks here. If the toys are going to be thrown out or are going to the op shop, it's best to put them in black garbage bags. I've been caught before when I put some toys in white garbage bags and the kids just happened to see through the plastic, and then I had to have a whole conversation about why those toys were being thrown out. Unless you are really good at hiding, I would also suggest not selling the toys at your garage sale. For the most part, the kids will have no interest in why all those strange people are in the front yard. They might even be oblivious to the fact you're having a garage sale. But if they happen to wander out and see their 'beloved' toys being sold, well, you might (again) be asking for a tantrum.

The other reason I advocate for getting rid of 50 to 75 per cent of the kids' toys is this: what occurs once a year, every year? Their birthday. And what occurs at the end of every year? Christmas. And what do they get on these occasions? More toys! It's never ending.

To control the amount of toys the kids have, I suggest getting a toy box (if you don't have one already). All their toys go into this. You can keep it at whatever percentage you want, but maybe look at keeping it between 50 and 75 per cent full. If it hits 100 per cent (or if you can't close the lid), then something's got to go. (And just to be clear, if one toy box gets filled, it doesn't mean buying another toy box!)

The other good thing about a toy box is that this is where *all* the toys are kept. OK, the kids might have one or two on display in their rooms and this is perfectly fine, but for the rest, they are kept in one place.

Obviously, things like ride-on toys or sporting equipment aren't going to fit in the toy box, and this is where you're going to have to use your own judgement. But I will ask this: do the kids have multiple ride-on toys? Do they really use all of them? Do they have multiple tennis balls, or multiple footballs, or multiple any type of sport balls? Are they using all of them? Have some been used to death? Are some flat and dead? Use your own judgement in regards to what needs **Rule #1** and **Rule #2** applied to them.

STEP 3: CLEAN IT

You've completed: **Throw It.**

You've completed: **Sort It.**

Now it's time to: **Clean It.**

And what is '**Clean It**', I hear you ask. Clean the room, you know, give it a good vacuum (or mop). Do a little dusting (or damp cloth wipe). Maybe let off an air freshener! It doesn't have to be too much, just enough to give it a nice fresh feel.

After you've decluttered a room and given it a quick clean, take a moment and bask in what you've accomplished. Soon your whole house will feel like this. Doesn't it feel good?

I told you that step would be quick! Now you can move on to your next room.

THE GARAGE SALE

You've used **Rule #1** to declutter your house. You've used **Rule #2** to declutter your house. Out of **Rule #2** you've decided to have a garage sale. When it comes to garage sales, I'm no expert, but I can offer some advice.

A piece of cardboard with *Garage Sale* shoddily handwritten in a thin black marker and stuck up on a pole is not going to attract all the buyers your garage sale could attract. It's hard to read that type of sign even driving past at slow speeds, let alone while drivers are concentrating on the traffic. Here is an example of what you should do.

Print out three pieces of A4 paper:

Paper 1)	First line:	GARAGE
	Second line:	SALE
Paper 2)	First line:	THE DAY & DATE
	Second line:	TIME
Paper 3)		ARROW (pointing the way)

Then stick the three pieces of paper to a piece of cardboard and attach it to a pole. If you want to get fancier, you could attach the cardboard to a dowel rod or garden post and hammer it into the ground. And if you want to get even more fancier, have signs on both sides of the post (just remember to have the arrows pointing in the right direction.) Also remember that depending on where you live, you may need multiple signs to guide drivers to your house. (And don't forget to remove the signs when your garage sale has ended.)

If you can, put the items for sale on a table or tables as it's a lot more comfortable for buyers to look at items this way. But if you can't do this, don't worry; on the ground is just fine.

You can put prices on the items, or if you want to be lazy, put all items for one dollar under one sign, all items for two dollars under another, etc., etc. If you don't want to do any pricing, when someone asks you 'how much' you either give them a price or ask them how much they would like to pay. Also remember, your prices are flexible; at the end of the time, you don't want anything left.

Saturday is the day most people will be out looking at garage sales.

If you can, pick a nice day to have the garage sale. If it's going to be monsoon season for the next two months then maybe you don't have a choice! But if at the start of the week the weather on Saturday is going to be nice but by Friday it's changed to being wet, put the garage sale off until it's nice again.

Professional garage sale buyers are out early. If this suits you then set up early. If it doesn't suit you, there is nothing wrong with starting at 9 am, 10 am, or even 11 am; just be ready for people to come at the time you have advertised.

Unless you want to be outside all day, don't have your garage sale run all day. Pick how many hours you want to spend on it and stick to that. I would suggest two to four hours at the minimum.

Have some notes and coins for change. You aren't a bank and most people who are buying at garage sales will have appropriate money. If someone comes along with only a 20-dollar note for a two-dollar item, they either come back or you tell them, 'You've got a nice face so you can have it for free!'

Finally, any items that haven't sold don't go back into the house! They are either thrown out or they go to the op shop (again, only if they are clean, undamaged and of good quality).

WHEN TO DECLUTTER

Now!

'Now?' Yes, now. Right now! You've read the three steps. You've got the two rules in hand, off you go. Go on!

OK, well, maybe I'm being a bit too pushy, but my point stands. Set aside an hour today or tonight (or tomorrow if you're reading this in bed and this guide is helping you go to sleep!) and start. You can start decluttering and continue reading this guide at the same time. The key though, is to just start.

Moving

Before a move is a *great* time to declutter. You will be packing up *everything* you own so why not **Rule #1** and **Rule #2** your items as you pack? If you plan your time, you can still organise a garage sale before you move, or you could decide to forego the garage sale (if you don't have the time) and items that were destined for the garage sale now go either into the garbage or to the op shop.

If, however, the timeframe you have for moving is short (maybe your landlord has decided to move back into the property or you've been offered a job and you need to move ASAP), you can still **Rule #1** and **Rule #2** your items as you pack, BUT, instead of appointing a large proportion of your thoughts to decluttering, appoint 20 per cent or 10 per cent; any small amount will do. You will at least do *some* decluttering at this opportune time.

Even if you had time to declutter before the move, or if you only had a little time to declutter before the move, or if you had *no* time to declutter before the move, guess what you can do when you arrive at the new property? **Rule #1** and **Rule #2** your items as you unpack. Get the essentials sorted first: bed/s, couch, TV, fridge, cutlery and kitchenware, clothes and toiletries, and whatever else you deem to be 'essential', then **Rule #1** and **Rule #2** the rest of your items as you unpack them.

Carpets, Painting or Renovating

The idea here is that as you're going to be moving the majority of your items to accommodate the house improvement task you're undertaking, why not declutter in the lead-up?

For the most part, people will just move their items, do the task and then move their items back to the same spot without giving any thought as to whether they really need to keep those items or not. The house will look great with new carpets or a fresh coat of paint or the new renovation, but it will still feel cluttered.

Increase the allocated timeframe for the house improvement task to be completed to include decluttering. When the task is complete, the house will not only look great but will be decluttered as well.

Kids Move Out

Somewhere between 'they're moving out for the first time' and 'they're definitely not moving back', is a good time to declutter (I'll leave the choice of timeframe up to you). You might still have old bikes, toys, school books or old hobby items that even the kids haven't seen or used in years.

As each kid leaves the nest, and if they're definitely not moving back, go through the declutter process with them and their items. If there is anything they are not taking with them, is there any good reason for it to be kept? Is there any good reason for it to remain at *your* house?

Retirement

If you've never decluttered in your life, or if you've only attempted it once or a few times over a 45-year period (moving out of home at 20, retiring at 65), retirement is another great time to declutter.

Hopefully you're not as busy in retirement as you were in your work life so you can really focus on decluttering your house (in between your other retirement activities of course!).

If your retirement consists of moving into a retirement village or downsizing, look at it as we discussed in '**Moving**'. But to be honest, for most people, you're going to have to declutter hard. I'd (almost!) put money on it that when you get into the retirement village or smaller house, you will still have too many items for the space. As you unpack though, if you become aware that you do have too many items, at least you can apply **Rule #2** to them.

End of Life

'Ninety-eight per cent of us will die at some point in our lives...' is one of my all-time favourite movie lines. (*Talladega Nights: The Ballad of Ricky Bobby*) You just can't argue with that percentage!

The reality is, the older we get the closer we get to death knocking on our door. (Well, for at least 98 per cent of us anyway!) And when we're gone, *someone else* is going to be going through our stuff deciding what will go into the garbage, what will be going to the op shop and what *they* will be keeping.

Decluttering may not be possible if your level of health is low or your level of sickness is high. But if you are capable, or have trusted family or friends who can help you, or it's just something you'd like to do, this time of life can be a good time to declutter. Especially when *you* can pass on items to whom or where *you* want them to go.

THE ADVANCED SECTION

If this is the 'Advanced Section', then I guess everything before this is the 'Basic Section'! It would probably be more apt to say that this is the 'Extra Section'. But I'm going to stick with 'Advanced'!

95 Per Cent

Your goal is to have each room (and section, and cupboard, and drawer, and shelf) at 95 per cent or less capacity. 'Oh! All those items I threw out and sold and gave to the op shop, and now you're telling me I can have a room full up to 95 per cent?', I hear you say. My response is: clearly you didn't need or want those items you've just thrown out because, drum roll please, you threw them out! You made the realisation that all those items were unnecessary and that is the realisation I want you to have.

And look, 95 per cent is just a number. Some of your rooms will be at 95 per cent capacity, some will be at 80 per cent, some at 70, some at 60—you get my point.

One time when I was single and living alone, I lived in a two-bedroom unit. The second bedroom had *nothing* in it. The second bedroom cupboard had an empty suitcase and a portable AC in it. If I had to guess the percentage of what my items took up in the rest of the unit, I'd have to say around 20 to 30 per cent. It wasn't that I was poor (thank goodness), it's just I am a minimalist and I loved walking into a practically empty house. Now I'm married with two kids, I'm still a minimalist, but my percentages have increased.

And I'll make a confession: our medicine container is 100 per cent full! 'Gasp,' I hear, 'how can we trust him now?' What I'll also tell you is that the 40 cm x 25 cm x 20 cm plastic container (bought from a hardware store) fits *very* neatly, *on* a shelf, *in* a cupboard. So while it is at 100 per cent capacity, the percentage is *offset* by the fact that it is stored neatly and out of sight.

You need to find your 'percentages', and find them for each room. Find what works for you. Stop, however, living at 100 per cent or higher capacity. Give yourself, your family and your house room to breathe. You'll feel better for it.

Partners

Consult with your husband / wife / girlfriend / boyfriend / partner / housemate / significant other (cats and dogs need not be consulted!) before you start your declutter journey. I mean, you can do the first step-**Throw It**-there's no recourse there.

I will, however, recommend you do this one thing: mention that you have read an amazing how-to guide! Tell them it's about decluttering and it's something *you'd* like to do, and it's something you'd like *them* to do *with* you.

100 Per Cent On-board

With any luck they'll be 100 per cent on-board. You'll work together on it, and live happily (decluttered) ever after.

Moderately On-board

If they are moderately on-board, lead by example; they'll probably jump on-board soon enough as they see the benefits. But until they are fully on-board, do not declutter items that are clearly 'theirs', like clothes, books, CDs, DVDs, games, their favourite chair (that you absolutely hate), anything that in a court of law they would claim was theirs. Begin the declutter process with only what is clearly yours.

If there is ambiguity as to what is 'theirs' and what is 'yours', then this is where you can shine with what you've learned. With **Rule #1** in hand, try something like this, 'Hey, <significant other>. This <insert the name of what you are holding>, I haven't used in the last 12 months. I don't imagine I'll use it in the next 12 months. I'd like to [**Rule #2**] throw it out / sell it / give it to the op shop, what do you think?'

Hopefully, they'll be surprised that some money may be made by selling some items. (We'll scare them with the prospect of a garage sale later!) Or they'll realise that there is a lot more around the house that could be gotten rid of and they'll join you in the process. You'll work together on it, and live happily (decluttered) ever after!

Not On-board (at All!)

If, however, they are 110 per cent *not* on-board, and it's not that they are violent about it (or maybe they are and in that case you may need to get out of there), but if there is an aggressive reaction, I would *strongly* recommend not decluttering. The process will have nil effect and may even dissuade you from decluttering in the future.

It might be time for you to think about how you can live happily (decluttered) ever after.

Foresight

After you've finished decluttering, you get a real sense of what needs to be kept in your house and what doesn't. It should naturally follow then (though this make take some time) that when you are considering purchasing something, you can reference **Rule #1** with a slight adjustment: 'Am I going to use it more than once in the next 12 months?'

Let's say you're at a whitegoods store and you're passing by the popcorn machines. You think, *A popcorn machine would be great. We can have fresh popcorn when we watch movies together. Oh, and this one doesn't use oil so it's healthier.* So you make your purchase, get it home with the intention of using it every week. By the end of 12 months, you realise it got taken out of the cupboard only once or twice because the microwave popcorn you buy at the supermarket is so much easier, quicker and tastes better!

Let's look at it another way. You're at the whitegoods store and you're passing by the popcorn machines. You think, *A popcorn machine would be great. We can have fresh popcorn when we watch movies together. Oh, and this one doesn't use oil so it's healthier.* But another thought comes into your head. *I've just decluttered my house. Do I really need to buy this machine? Is this machine going to clutter up my cupboard?* So you go home and Friday movie night comes along. You think to yourself, *Some popcorn would be nice*, but you don't have a machine. Then the following Friday movie night comes along. Again you think, *Some popcorn would be nice*, but you don't have a machine and, further yet, you don't actually like supermarket microwave popcorn. In this instance, when you ask yourself, 'Am I going to use it more than once in the next 12 months?', you can reasonably expect that, indeed, you are going to use the appliance many times in the next 12 months and therefore purchasing this appliance will not add clutter to your house.

Another aspect to foresight is: when something is about to be bought or comes into the house, does it need to be kept? This is particularly applicable when the kids bring items home from school or friends offer to give you something.

When our kids bring home notices from school, if it's for an event we aren't going to attend, the notice goes straight into the recycling bin; there's no time for that notice to clutter up anything. If it's an excursion, the notice is kept until the date of the excursion and then it goes into the recycling bin. If it's a piece of art, well, we've already talked about the kids' art. Is it going to replace any existing art in the house or is it going to be thrown out? Foresight helps with these decisions.

When family or friends offer to give you something, ranging from a piece of furniture down to a book, because you've decluttered the house, you can ask yourself, 'This thing that my friend or family member wants to give me, do I really need it? Am I really going to use it? Is this thing just going to clutter up my house?' You'd be surprised when you think, with decluttering in mind, how many things you will turn away because you can see with foresight that you won't or don't actually need them.

Maintenance

Foresight will help you keep your house decluttered, but some time down the track, you will notice that you've let things get through your 'declutter net'. I'm not even an exception to this! My hope, of course, is that you don't need to do another full house declutter. Any further declutters past your first one should take only a fraction of your time.

You may notice that one of the bedside table drawers has accumulated some things and it's only a matter of putting those things back where they belong. You may notice that your plastics cupboard has hit 100 or 105 per cent capacity and it just needs a quick declutter. Maybe you've collected a few medications in the last 12 months that you no longer require. Maybe you did accept a piece of furniture from a friend or family member that you thought you were going to use but it turns out you haven't. It'll be quick for you to declutter it.

Maintaining your declutter is an ongoing process, but it's not a hard one. Just keep that declutter word tucked in the back of your mind and hopefully it will become second nature to you.

Breaking Rule #1

Yep, I've just written a whole guide about decluttering and here I am advocating breaking **Rule #1**! But before you get the sense that you've wasted your money and time, I want to give you a few examples of where breaking **Rule #1** is perfectly acceptable.

Glasses

I have an old pair of glasses and an old pair of sunglasses in one of my bedside drawers. Both are prescription and I haven't worn them in years. But, if something happens to either of my regular glasses, I have backups.

My TV has a 3D option (remember that phase?). I have two pairs of 3D glasses that I've used once or twice but I don't think I'll ever use again. So why am I breaking **Rule #1**? In the first case, the drawer that they are in has our gaming console controllers and those glasses; the drawer is only 10 per cent full. Second, I'm not the gamer in the family so I never use that drawer. (I forgot they were in there until I wrote this section!) When I move I'll get rid of them, but until then there's no harm in breaking **Rule #1** for them.

Suits

I have one suit. It hangs up in a cover bag at the back of our walk-in-wardrobe. I'm lucky in that my body shape hasn't changed that much in the past five years, and in the last five years I've worn the suit to two weddings and one funeral. I don't see, in the foreseeable future, that I will need to wear it again, but it's good to have there just in case. There's no harm in breaking **Rule #1** for it.

The idea of breaking **Rule #1** isn't so you can hang on to anything that needs to be thrown out. It's about understanding that there are exceptions to any rule as long as you aren't throwing the basis of the rule out altogether or using it as an excuse to keep anything that needs to go.

Plastic Containers

Plastic containers are great to store items in but I'm not saying throw everything in plastic containers and then don't throw anything out. As I mentioned earlier, we keep most of our medications in a plastic container in the cupboard. It keeps them in one place and keeps them neat. I have a small lunchbox-sized container that I keep our spare batteries in. My wife has a plastic container that she keeps her sewing items in. We have a small plastic container that we keep our spare stationery in. Plastic containers aren't some type of magical force field that **Rule #1** and **Rule #2** can't get too. Apply the rules to everything you have in your plastic containers as well.

Collections

Wow. Aren't I going to step into a minefield here!

You can probably guess that I'm not a collector, but I'm not going to tell anyone that they can't be. The advice I will offer is: keep it proportional to the available space you have, and display it neatly.

If you collect items that are small, then allocation of space isn't so hard. It's easy to find a shelf or two to keep your collection on, or a container to keep you collection in. As your collection increases in size, the amount of space you allocate either needs to increase or you need to make some decisions about what will stay in the collection and what will go.

Whatever space you have for your collection, keep it displayed neatly; this is how to keep it decluttered, and it allows you to enjoy your collection. If you've stuffed all of it into a space, and if each piece has no 'room to breathe', how can you enjoy your collection? It will look cluttered and it will feel cluttered. Declutter it and the collection will serve its purpose; to be visually enjoyable.

My final advice on collections is: if it's packed away in a box somewhere and hasn't seen the light of day in years, then what's the point of keeping it? In most cases, collections are to be visually observed. If they can't or haven't been then let's make an adjustment to **Rule #1**: 'Have I viewed my collection in the last 12 months? Will I view my collection in the next 12 months?' If the answer is 'no', then maybe apply **Rule #2** to it.

Fixers

I'm not saying you *can't* fix the broken item you are keeping, you might be a well-skilled fixer, but will you fix it in an *appropriate* time? Has it been sitting in your house (garage or shed) for days? Weeks? Months? (And please don't tell me it's been years!) Has your partner been nagging you about getting it fixed, or simply about just throwing it out? What's worse: would a paid professional have fixed it in a timely manner and for an amount far below what your time is worth? Or, would it have been cheaper (and easier) to just go buy a new one? Think about these questions and decide whether the items you're intending to fix need to be kept or need to be decluttered.

For those of you who are hobby fixers, the decluttering process is a little different. For you, the time you spend fixing things is your alone time, your rest time, your 'get away from the world (or partner)' time. What I would have you consider though is: how many 'projects' do you have on the go? If you have a shed or garage or room full of broken items that need to be fixed, *realistically*, how many will you have time to fix, and, *realistically*, how many will you be able to fix? If you've got kids and full-time work and time to fix just one item in the year, then keep one item and declutter the rest. It's not too hard finding more items to fix! At the other end of the spectrum, if you're retired and you spend your days fixing items, maybe having a shed, garage or room full of broken items isn't a problem. But is there anything that is just rubbish? Is there anything that you don't enjoy fixing? Maybe you could declutter down to half of what you have? Be *realistic* about what you can achieve with your hobby, and declutter the rest.

Garage/Shed

I should include the garage or shed as one of the rooms, but I wanted you to focus on the inside of the house first, as that's where you spend most of your time. I'll focus on two areas: storage and tools.

A garage will usually have the overflow from the house and items that are in 'storage'. Again, you need to ask yourself whether you are storing your items for good reason or just because you don't want to throw them out. Maybe **Rule #1** them and then ask it again but with a small adjustment: 'Have I used it in the last two years? Am I going to use it in the next two years? Have I used it in the last three years? Am I going to use it in the next three years? Have I used it in the last four years? Am I going to use it in the next four years?' The further your timeframe extends, the more that the item probably isn't needed, and then you apply **Rule #2** to it.

Then, second, tools. And tools is a hard one. You can have a tool that you haven't used in years and then, suddenly, bam! you need it. And chances are you'll use it that one time and not need it again for another few years, but because of the cost of it, you wouldn't buy a new one each time you needed it. I bought a carpet cleaner a couple of years ago. Did the whole house over one weekend and it's been sitting in the shed ever since. It definitely doesn't meet **Rule #1**, but there is no way I'll be decluttering it because it's a great tool and I know eventually I will use it again.

If you can't even get into your garage or shed to get a tool because it's so full, then you need to declutter it. If you can't even use your workbench because it is 110 per cent over capacity, then you need to declutter. The choice is really easy. You either apply **Rule #2** to your tools, or you organise them. Again, I don't want to be sending you out to purchase containers and storage systems, but that might be an option that you use.

Outside

Throughout this guide I'm sure some of you have been thinking, *When do I declutter outside the house?* and others are now thinking, *I have to declutter outside the house?* Well, yes, of course! But if you only decluttered inside the house and didn't declutter the outside, I wouldn't be upset.

At the very least, mow your lawn and put away anything that has been left outside that belongs inside the house, inside the garage or inside the shed. Anything on top of that is a bonus!

Maybe you've got some fairy lights that no longer work. Take them down and throw them out. Maybe you've got some plants that have well and truly died. Throw them out. Maybe you've got too many pot plants and they make the outside of the house look cluttered; maybe it's time to declutter those. Maybe there's a vine on your fence that was there before you moved in and you've always hated it. Maybe now is the time to take action on it.

While I believe decluttering the outside of your house isn't as important as decluttering the inside, it's still nice when it's done!

Junk Mail

Put a 'No Junk Mail' or a 'No Advertising Mail' sign on your letterbox. I see no good reason *not* to have one on it.

There are three things with junk mail: 1) By its nature alone, it adds clutter to your house. 2) It goes from your mail box directly to your recycle bin without you even looking at it. 3) It 'informs' you of things that you probably don't need to buy in the first place.

The sign won't rid your house of 100 per cent of the junk mail, but 95 to 99 per cent junk mail declutter is pretty good.

Storage Units

There are a few legitimate reasons to have a storage unit. Maybe you're building a new house, and originally there was a crossover period between selling the old house and moving into the new house, but there's been a delay and you've had to move temporarily into a small rental. You've got to keep your items somewhere. Maybe a parent or grandparent has passed away and you've got a limited timeframe to organise their items. Maybe you don't have the space in your house for the extra items. You've got to keep the items somewhere. Maybe you're travelling for six or 12 months. You've got to keep your items somewhere.

'Because you have too many items and your house is too full' is not a legitimate reason to have a storage unit. I'm sure the storage unit industry makes half its money from customers who are storing their items rather than working out whether **Rule #1** or **Rule #2** apply to them.

Documents

I did hesitate putting this item in because decluttering your documents is a process all in itself. In fact, I don't even mind if you skip it! Yep, that's right, in fact, I *want* you to skip it! Go on. Jump ahead to the **CONCLUSION** and come back when you've decluttered your house and you've had at least a month of rest from decluttering.

...

...

For those of you who didn't take my advice, we'll keep going. And for those who did, welcome back!

Documents, like everything else, need to be decluttered. The problem is they aren't governed by **Rule #1** or **Rule #2**: 'Have I used this document in the last 12 months? Am I going to use this document in the next 12 months? Is it garbage, going into the garage sale, to the op shop, or is it staying?'

The other reason why I hesitated to add this section was because I want you to go buy yourself a filing cabinet (that is if you haven't got one already). As I've mentioned elsewhere, I don't want your decluttering to be contingent on having to buy things to have it be successful. In regards to documents though, a filing cabinet is your best success to declutter them. And it doesn't have to be a three- or four-drawer one. You could probably just get a one-drawer one, although I do recommend getting a two-drawer one just in case one drawer is just that little bit too small. (Also, the top drawer can be A–K and the bottom drawer L–Z, just to spread files out a bit. Again, giving the filing cabinet some 'breathing' room.) You'll also need to buy yourself a pack of suspension files. (Personally, I'd buy two packs, although if it's not a hassle for you to visit a stationery store, start with one pack.) The suspension files should come with tabs and, of course, you can buy the coloured ones if you want to get a bit fancy!

The other key to decluttering documents is solid, uninterrupted thinking time. If the kids are at home and aren't settled into what they are doing, being interrupted every five minutes isn't going to produce a successful declutter result. If your favourite TV show is on and you think you can do both at the same time, well, I can tell you which one will win out. (Hint: it's not the decluttering!) Chances are, this is going to take more than an hour or two, so set aside a good block of uninterrupted time (or a couple of blocks of uninterrupted time) to get this task done.

To start, attach the tabs to the suspension files and mark the labels. You might have: bank, business, electricity, gas, medical adult, medical kids, mortgage, pets, receipts, rent, school, tax, warranties, water ... I'll leave the categories up to you. Next, you want to set up an area where you can have all the suspension files laid out (maybe a table or the floor, and you can decide whether you lay them out open or closed). Then it's a matter of grabbing a bunch of documents and sorting them into the appropriate suspension file. That seems easy enough! Well, remember, this is a guide about decluttering not just 'sorting'. You still don't want to keep documents that don't need to be kept.

For those of you who already have a filing cabinet and file your documents away regularly, this task will be a bit easier. You can select one suspension file at a time, declutter it, then move onto the next. I still recommend, though, that you set aside a good block of uninterrupted time to declutter your documents.

And I'll add here again: what documents you throw out is up to you. I'm only making suggestions. If you aren't sure if a document should be thrown out or not, don't spend five minutes trying to work it out, keep it and decide next time you declutter if it's time for it to be thrown out.

- Do you need to keep every bank statement or just the last one? Do you even need to keep the last one? All your statements should be available online, so do you need to keep them? Or old documents from a bank you're no longer with. Do you need to keep any of those?
- Your tax documents only need to be kept for a certain number of years. Do you need to keep ones going further back than that?
- You might still have vet documents from a pet that passed away some time ago. Do you need to keep any of that?
- Are there receipts that you've kept that are now faded and you can't read them? They can be thrown out. Are there receipts for items that you no longer have? They can be thrown out.
- Do you need to keep your paid utilities bills? Maybe keep just the last few?
- If you have servicing records, registration records and any other documents for a car you sold some time ago, do they need to be kept?
- With insurance documents, obviously keep the most current, but do you need to keep anything further back than that?

- Maybe there is a bunch of primary school documents but your kids are in high school now. Do you need to keep them?

To be honest, I'll think you'll be surprised at how many documents you've accumulated that you don't actually need to keep. I know after you declutter them, your filing cabinet is going to feel better for it!

CONCLUSION

At the end of this guide, I have this advice:

1) Declutter at your own, but regular, pace.

2) Declutter one room (or section) at a time.

3) Don't cause yourself to become overwhelmed while decluttering.

4) After you've decluttered, enjoy the breathing space you have created.

All the best decluttering.

Andrew

QUICK REFERENCE

Throw It. Sort It. Clean It.

Rule #1

'Have I used it in the last 12 months?

Am I going to use it in the next 12 months?'

Rule #2

'Is it going into the garbage,

into your garage sale,

to the op shop, or is it staying?'

Made in the USA
Monee, IL
07 July 2026

56550064R00039